# Mr. Softy

# Mr. Softy

*Morton Lynn*

iUniverse, Inc.
New York  Lincoln  Shanghai

# Mr. Softy

iUniverse books may be ordered through booksellers or by contacting:

iUniverse
2021 Pine Lake Road, Suite 100
Lincoln, NE 68512
www.iuniverse.com
1-800-Authors (1-800-288-4677)

Because of the dynamic nature of the Internet, any Web addresses or links contained in this book may have changed since publication and may no longer be valid.

The views expressed in this work are solely those of the author and do not necessarily reflect the views of the publisher, and the publisher hereby disclaims any responsibility for them.

ISBN: 978-0-595-46513-2 (pbk)
ISBN: 978-0-595-90811-0 (ebk)

Printed in the United States of America

# MR SOFTEE

What do I know about writing a book?
Nothing ... Why bother....

I remember what school decentralization first came about in NYC. I was the representative for my children's public school. P.S. 184 in Queens. We used to meet in P.S.200. Murray Burgtrum was the president of the board. Gary Ackerman and I used to sit together. Big fight then was the Catholic Church wanted a book removed from the public library. "Down These Mean Streets." would you believe it.

Gary once said to me, "I think I will start a newspaper." I looked at him and said "What do you know about running a newspaper" nothing, but I know how to hire the right people. Anyone living in Queen s will remember the Queens Tribune. Gary must have gotten involved with politics and the next thing I heard he was running for Congress In case you do not know it he was elected twice so far. It is now Congressman Ackerman. He is also one of those rare politicians who remembers he came from. My wife was having trouble collecting her social security checks even though she was over 65. I eventually called his office in Washington. He was not in but I told his office what my problem, was. Within a week I got a letter from him, telling me he did remember me and he would see what he could do. Next thin g I knew my wife was getting her checks. Why am I telling you all this? I am, very fortunate in having an old(she will not like the word old) dear friend who is very good at this kind of work. She wrote as a kid in Public School, writes now for her local newspaper and the Princeton Paper and will continue writing forever. I will see if I can get her interested in doing my book. We have much history together, who knows where it will end up. I certainly will not be running for office

Why am I writing this book? I like to read autobiographies. I find them interesting but I can not relate to any I have read recently. I guarantee if you are between 65 and 80 you will find this book interesting. You will be familiar with some of the incidents I am sure we all went through similar experiences. Maybe more sex, but if you are in my age bracket it was different than today's relationships. We had to work at it.

I do not intend to change any of the names, maybe one or two to avoid any legal problems. You will know who I am talking about. I also do not know the limit on Rape charges so I will be careful I hope you enjoy reading this book as much as the fun I had remembering these 75 years. If any of our old club members from the Bronx should happen to read this book, JEMS, JAYS, TORCHES or the girl's clubs RENAH or UV'S call me I am in the book.

Introduction

# IN THE BEGINNING

Just finished reading Erica Jong's "Seducing the Demon" She had an interesting life but mine was more exciting and easier to relate to.

I think I'll write a book all about my life. I will get Phyllis to edit it and correct the English. Who is Phyllis you ask? She is an old(she will not like the word old) girlfriend from 60 years ago. She had a big crush on me in both Public and high School. Sorry I didn't take advantage of it. That was different times, different values. My mother did a job on me. "You do not take advantage of the opposite sex". Now 60 years later I will try a new ... I will wait till she finishes my book first

Lets see, where do you begin. Born in Atlantic City 5/22/31. My mom went home to give birth. It was a much different Atlantic city then. My father was a NY hot shot, they were first cousins no less. He was a good salesman or my mom wanted to get away from AC. I do not know which is correct, but, she sure made a mistake. My mom Lillian had too much to give and did not get it back from my father Harry. She had so much love to give, that when my brother Norm went into the Navy, my mom took in a foster child. Probably partly my fault as I was very independent and you could do nothing for me. Judy my foster sister was 11 months when we got her. Her mother had died when she was very little and her father Had a elder mother he was taking care of and he could not handle both. He was a good father and never missed a visiting day. Unfortunately for us his mother died and he remarried. He took Judy back on her 5th birthday. Boy was that traumatic for all of us. My friends still ask about her. We were very close. I used to take her with me all the time. All she had to do was Ask for anything and she got it. My mom made her an early 5<sup>th</sup> birthday party. Everybody was there, family friends, neighbors. What a crying jag we had after she left. The social worker told us the best thing we could do was not try and see her. I foolishly listened. There is Jewish word Bershert. Literally it means it was meant to be. Well Judy's new family lived accross the street from my cousin Gladys on Featherbed lane in the Bronx. I made my friend Julie(He had a car) drive me around the neighborhood trying to get a look at her. Did get together with Judy later in life. First time we just sat and cried. Judy is doing veery well married to Bernie and they have two daughters. She is a grandmother now and we have plans to see each other for lunch April 2007.

Back to my life. Since my mom grew up in AC and her whole family was there, for the first 14 years of my life I spent every holiday and summer in AC.

My mom had three brothers. The middle one Edwards was called Cecil(nick name came from coal company. he worked at Cecil coal) He got involved with Gambling casino in town. Oh you didn't know they had gambling casino in town back then? I remember he once took me with him to pick up his girlfriend Florence. She was a show girl on the Boardwalk. It was the first time I saw very long finger nails and a big brim hat. She was gorgeous He eventually married her and my grandfather sat Shiva … Yes she was a shiksa. My aunt Florence passed away in 2006 she was 90 and still gorgeous. After we took her home we went to I think it was called the 500 club. I know it was on Arkansas ave diagonally across from the train station. I remember, Thick plush red carpets. At least a dozen dice tables, black jack tables but I do not remember many slot machines. I do remember the girls selling cigars and cigarettes. Wit their short skirts. One of the owners was Nucky Johnson big time gambler. Little Johnny from "CALL FOR PHILLIP MORRIS" was also involved, remember him? Always wondered why they did not have a problem wit the police. I had my own problems

Had to find work. You could not get working papers until you were 13. Next year. My first job same as everyone else had. I delivered a free newspaper to all of Chelsea Heights. Never heard of it? It ran from the High School on Albany ave to the bridge on Dorset ave the start of Ventnor. I made $4 Would buy a hot pie for $2. One thing good about the job was that I was home by 8AM I'll bet a lot of you had the same job. When I got back to the Terrace my friend Vincent was waiting for me.(separate story on the terrace). We would go all around town and pick up the big fruit and vegetable baskets the store keepers wanted to get rid of. We did this all summer long. Why? Do you remember the Beauty Pagaent? All the contestants would ride down the boardwalk till Convention Center on Georgia Ave. We would sell the baskets to the spectators. I think we charge .25 each. We thought we were rich. I know we always had more than 200 baskets by the time the parade was in Sept.

Next summer I had my working papers and I got a real job at MRS Smiths Bath House. I think it was on the Boardwalk at North CarolinaAve. People used to come to the beach for the day and rent lockers to change clothes. There was only one other boy working with me. He was a year or two older. This was a fun job. We drilled holes in the roof of several lockers, when a pretty girl came in we would give her one of these lockers. We would take turns running upstairs to watch her change her clothes. I especially liked girls with big boobs(funny how taste changes, today anything over a hand full is wasted) I know they put someting in the milk for the next generation. Rarely did we have a big busted girl unless she was fat. I got tired of looking at breasts so I changed my job. Next job I was an Entrepreneur. Place was a hot dog stand part of the 5& 10 cent store also on the Boardwalk. This was not a regular hot dog stand. I would put the hot dog in a slot, pour batter all around it and bake the dog in the roll. It took less than 5 minutes. Only thing bad about this job was I had to come in before the store opened up and skin all the hot dogs2-300 per day. I got even with them and did my Christmas shopping in the store before it opened. I saved a lot of money that summer. I think I bought $200 worth of clothes when I got home. Only thing bad was my brother got discharged from the Navy and he fit into my clothes.

I think I told you my mom had three brothers., youngest one was only 13 years older than me. Harris called Hesh. I worked with him one summer. We had a linen route. Small hotels and rooming houses rented their linens. We would deliver clean and take away the dirty ones after counting them. Didn't think it was necessary to wear gloves in those days. I remember one stop in a Black neighborhood we stopped twice a week. We collected over 200 hand towels and only few sheets each time we went there. Wonder what they did.? Hesh also had a favorite stop. He was interested in the daughter of one of the rooming houses we stopped at. He eventually married her Esther and they moved to Calif. I still see one of their daughters Doni. Doni sand Dave are tennis buffs and they come to NY for the open. They always make it their business to see me, either in the Hamptons or in the City. See picture of Doni with my brother and our wives in front of LeCirc. (Am sure I spelled that wrong).

Oldest brother Nate had it rought. He had to quit school when he was in the ninthgrade I think and go to work. He really had a head for business. I think when that happens you try harder. He owned a Coal company, Garage, Two automobile agencies and a truck agency. He the got involved with Al Moskowitz and they started buying up all the land the hotels were on. Their combine owned it all. They also owned the land on the Bayside. He was suppose to let me get involved with one of the deals but he never did. He was so busy with business that he neglected his family. His daughter Sue got married young and moved to Cincinnati where her husband skip came from. See Sue on the beach and in family pictures. His son Mark he pushed so hard that he had a nervous breakdown. It cost my Uncle Nate a small fortune. Mark ended up in Hillsdie Hospital in Queen s. He was there two years at $320 a day. Ros and I used to take Mark home to AC on weekends. I will never forget one weekend Ros came into his parents house with her arm around him. That night aun t Sally said to Ros "youdid that so easy I could not put my arm around him like that" All the money does not do you any good if you can not feel.

Some pictures in the book. Me on top of Hesh, my brother below. Sue and me at 10. Picture of my Mom's parents 50<sup>th</sup> anniversary party at the Breakers hotel only one that was kosher. Grandparents with us Sue is in the middle of my brother and I with our wives. Uncle Nate in front with my grandparents

# LIBERTY TERRACE

That's where my Grandparents lived. What a great place. Monopoly players will know where it is and the financial status of the neighborhood. It is on Fairmont Ave between Florida and Georgia Ave. Fairmont is below Arctic Ave closer to the Bay. My Mom and all her brothers lived there. Four blocks to the Boardwalk where Convention Center was.

The Terrace Had twelve homes. 6 on each side. See pictures. When my mom was growing up the terrace was all Jewish. By the time I got there it was all Italian except for my grandparents. These were real Italians. If a husband died the widow wore black the rest of her life. They all grew their own grapes and made their own wine. I used to be able to talk Italian but it's all gone now. I even went to church Sunday, morning. St Michaels on Missouri Ave. The father even knew me by name. We really had a ball. Let's see #2 Germanno Family 4 boys and one girl. My uncle Hesh used to take out the girl Clementine. She was a nice looking head Boys, Russell, Anthony, Horrace and I can not remember the youngest ones name. Next door was the LaVerdi's Charlie was the oldest and my best friend. He had three sisters Grace, Rochetta, and Delia. They had a cousin living with them, I think he lost his parents Raymond. #6 was a women with a big dog. We were all afraid of her. #8 Andellora's Charlie and Vincent my business partner. Last one on that side was an old German couple who kept feeding us candy. Other side of the Terrace #3 was a lady who lived alone, never had any visitors, or spoke to anyone. #5 wasthe firstr Macagnano Family. Two sisters and a brother. Mary, Mamie and Paul. I sawthem about 6 years ago.

Paul has a beauty parlor on Ventnor Ave near Margate. I went in with my daughter in law Janet. He recognized me immediately. He has not seen me in over 50 years. Paul is a concilman in Ventnor and he told me if I get a ticket to give it to him. I guess the town has not changed much. His sister Mamie was in one of the chairs and she recognized me too. I used to have a crush in his sister Mary. My son who lives outside Philadelphia rents a house in Marvin Gardens during the summer, that's how I got there. Where was I #7. that was my grandparents house. I guess my brother spent a lot of time there also. Judy spent a few summers there also. I remember she had a habit of putting her finger in her mouth with a ring on. You guessed it she swallowed the ring. Actually it got stuck in her throat. We could not get it out. My old fashioned grandmother. Put her finger in her mouth and pushed the ring down. We were all nervous wrecks until we found it in her bowl movement that night. I asked Judy if her girls do the same thing but she said no. Lets see #9 the other Macagnnano family,. Brothers.One son and three girls plus a cousin who lived with them Girls, Clementine, Sadie, Pauline and Paul #2. Can not remember cousins name but she is the tallest one in picture of the girls from the Terrace. Cannot remember who lived in 11. I guess I was wrong only 10 house in the Terrace.

Plenty of kids all within 5-6 years of each other. We played all kinds of games. War, hide the beans, and wire ball. I'll bet you never played wire ball. We would throw a ball up in the air, try and hit the overhead wire and call out someones name. And run. When you got the ball you had to hit someone with it. Better not try it today, the wire might break, we never thought it was a live wire. Socially they were years behind this NY Hot shot. I had to teach them how to play spin the bottle. Maybe they were better off. See pictures of Terrace. Vincent and Charlie with me, my mom. Pictures of girls, you can get an idea what the terrace looked like.

Next time you are in AC take a ride. Go down Florida Ave till it ends, go right on Fairmont, terrace is before you get to Georgia Ave,

My friends were always teasing me AC is another Coney Island. We were All newleweds. I took three couple. This was in 1952. We went for the weekend. We stayed at the Chelsea Hotel, It had an indoor pool in the basement. First I had them riding bikes on the Boardwalk. Next we went horseback riding on the beach. We went to a black nightclub. We were the only white people there. We closed the place down and till this day I do not think I have heard better jazz. I of course took them to the Whitehouse for subs. My son still takes people there. We also went to a grill on North Caroli-naAve. They used to make sandwiches like Juniors in Brooklyn It's gone now like a lot of other good places. The town is not the same and it is not for the best the change.

# *DIAMOND LIL*

MY Mom was one of a kind. I'll bet a lot of guy say that. Lillian didn't have diamonds, however when she entered a room the place lit up. In the Jewish tradition one of the highest honors you can give a person is to name your child after them. My mom's neighbors children named their kids after her. Two of my friends named their children after her as well. At her funeral every storekeeper from the neighborhood was there. There was 27 cars in her funeral procession. I still miss her. I think I told you what happened when my brother went into the Navy. Mom went down to Jewish Federation for Judy. We had the house all ready for her, but did we get a surprise. At 11 months Judy was drinking from a glass, no bottles and she was not sleeping in a crib. The agency gave you money but If I could have the money my mom spent on Judy's clothes I would be a richer man today. Recently my cousin Marilyn in Florida brought up the party we had for Judy before she left us. Her younger sister Alma is the one who started us all on a crying jag. I just realized I wrote about Judy already, this is about my mom. I have a few pictures of Judy in my arms and at the table. My mom catered to everyone. My friend Julie liked cherry soda. Nobody could touch his soda in the refrigerator. I am sure she kept something special for my friends Eric too. Phyllis kept a diary maybe she can give me some input. I know she told me she used to come to my house to practice her typing. I wish I had kept a diary. Later on I will tell you about my Navy days. One of my buddies Norm came from Calif. He became another member of my family He could not go home for the weekend so he came home with me. Even when I did not go home he did. I know he got better treatment than I did. I saw him in Calif about 15 years ago. First words out of his mouth was,"I told you I had a brother in NY" His daughters thought he was nuts. I'll send hi ma copy of this book.

They say if you leave a good name, you live on. Lillian sure will

# GROWING UP

**What a difference, when we came home from Public School the first ting we did was change our clothes. One thing I like about Parochial School is you have to come dressed. My grandson Remy goes to LaSalle a Catholic High School**. He has to wear a shirt and tie every day. They do not have to match and they usually do not. All his class rooms have a sign. "Boys Will Be Boys but LaSalle Boys Will be Gentlemen"

Had out milk and cookies and off to the school yard. Softball, basketball, handball and just bull shitting. I liked to play handball. I had a terrible crush on Iris, she was a pretty good handball player. I even let her win some of the games. Saw her recently and she still thinks she was better than me. I introduced her to her husband Eugene. He passed away about 6 years ago See picture of Monroe HS Reunion after 20 years. They are t3 and 4 on my right. Right next to them is Elaine and Morty, than May and Milty and Rita And Larry. They all come up later on. When you play Jewish Geography the world is smaller. Eugene is related to Elayne one of my wife's friends. Iris and Gene used to live in Roslyn area my cousin Carolyn 's daughter went to high school with one of their daughters Hm just thought of Iris again. Since she is a widow, I'll call her if things do not work out with Phyllis. Back to life then. We went to P.S 93 on Boynton Ave and Story ave. As boys we were a little wild. If you tore your pants it was OK as long as they were not school pants. I remember walking down Elder Ave. Eric had a bat in his hand, as we passed each window he would say yes or no. Yes meant a broken window. I think he broke about 6 windows that day. Jerry another friend and I was given a job in the school to restack books. We would stand at one end of the room and throw the books at the light switch. Jerry became a High School Chemistry teacher in Cardozza. My niece Lori had him one term and he also remembered the crazy things we did. Phyllis complained to me thatClifford was always putting her hair in the ink well. Ask your grandchildren if they know what an ink well is. That is the only things we did wrong. What sissy's we were

Next came High School. Most of us went to James Monroe three blocks up on Boynton Ave. All I can remember about High School is trying to make out. I had a crush on my math teacher Miss Seglow. It was her first job so she was probably about 20. She refused to go out with me but she did fix me up with her sister. Same family one was beautiful the other was OK. Can not say more still had to pass the class. I played the drums and I took every music course I could. Band. Orchestra, Music History, Major music and probably a few more. I was a typical wise guy. When graduation came, you had to list your accomplishments. I put down Girls Athletic Manager. If it wasn't for my good friends Dick and Cathy I would not have been in the book. They talked Mr Taub into letting me stay in the book They were Jimmy and Jamie Monroe two goody good shoes. I did manage to get out on time. Not much smarter than when I went in. I am sure you can see my English and Grammer errors. Thing I enjoyed most about High School was the proms. I went to three of them and had a great time. Always ended up on the Staten Island Ferry. Must confess did not do much scoring. See picture of me at my prom. I can not remember my dates name but I can remember exactly where she lived on Bryant Ave even the apartment number. She looked just like Debbie Reynolds

Off to work in the Mountains before the Navy

# PARTY TIME

I am 15 now and looking to work in the Mountains as a musician.

Mr drum teacher Sammy Ulano played in the Windsor Hotel in Fallsburg. His trumpet player also had a music school and they hooked us up with three guys. Jerry my trumpet player, Danny my saxophone player and Eugene our pianist. Eugene was a Julliard student. He was brilliant. We had our band. My house was the practice hall as I had a piano. I lived on the ground floor and we always had an audience. Who ever got the job was the band leader that night. We worked parties and became known as a very good Jewish band. We also worked an Irish Bar outside Bronx zoo. We became the house band. It always cost me a new set of Maracas after each affair. Everybody had to play them.

Our first job in the Mountains, Borsch Belt we used an Agent. Metzger and Bleiman they were big in those days They got us a job at the Alaben Hotel in Ellenville. The hotel was owned by two butchers from 170st in the Bronx. We really lucked out, we expected a dump to sleep in but they gave us a bungalow by the pool. Two bedrooms. I was hitting on a girl, Betty I think her name was. She is the one in the club sweater in the picture. Her mother was very protective. She kept yelling at me. Once she caught us kissing and she was furious. That night after work around 11PM we were sitting on the porch going over the nights work.

Uh oh. hear comes Betty's mother. The rest of the band went for a walk.

She grabs me by the arm and pulls me into the bedroom. She opens her robe and she is completely naked. Up comes my friend.

28

She said she will teach me how to treat a lady(some lady) I was 15 most I ever got was a feel. Naturally I reached a climax much too fast. She managed to get me up again. Again I came too fast. She was getting annoyed with me. She said she will tell me what to do. I couldn't even spell clitoris let alone know what to do to it. She was good, she showed me how to get her up to speed, and what she liked. I was a good student. She said all women would like what she taught me. She was correct but only one I had that much patience with was my wife. I was sure I would not forget that summer. I did promise to leave her daughter alone. At least not try and take her virginity. It was really a fun summer and I got paid for it. Pictures of the band, topsy turvy night and other photos of the group. No other excitement and could not wait til next summer.

Next summer we got our own job. Hotel in Hurleyville. Can not remember its name. You turn right by the post office in Monticello the hotel was about 5 miles up on the right. Was not so lucky that year. I did manage to get a girl from one of the bungalows into my room. We were both completely naked and she started to cry. She was a virgin. Mr Softee told her to getdressed. She never came back to the hotel after that. My Saxaphone player Danny met a girl from one of the bungalows. Eileen, she was 14. He fell in love with ehr and dated her till she was 17 and then they got married. We saw each other while our families were growing up but after a while we drifted away. My trumpet player became a patent lawyer. I am sure my piano played did something with his music as he was great. Plenty of times the acts came late and he read their music without a hitch. They all wanted to take him with them.

Last year we worked in the Mountains was the best. I do not remember how we got the job, but we were workingfor the night club not the. Hotel wasthe Flagler. Igave my friend Eric money tol take care of my girlfriend Rhoda. While I was away. When I came home they were engaged. Ericc was all of 17. You will understand later why I bring it up now. This job was classy and we had to get unifrms. We bought jackets on 23$^{rd}$ street. We looked professional. See picture. This was also the year latin music was big. We came up as a latin band. My name was Alvera Escobar. Since we were working for the concession, we got to eat in the main dinning room. It cost us more forTips than we were making. I think it was an 8 and 5 house. Thats $13 every week. I had a new girlfriend Flo Haber. Her father owned the candy store when you come out of croton park on the corner. Haber's. Do you know it? She came up for a couple of weekends and I knew I was not bringing any money home this summer. It was worth it. After work all the bands would end up at Cory's in Liberty. Machita, Tito Puenta, and all the dance teams were always there. You could buy Marijuanna sticks for .50 each. Solid and cut like a regular cigarette. I remember Killer Joe was the best customer. Boy could he dance. He came to our Band Night when we had it. Advantage of working for the nightclub was we were allowed 3 free drinks a night. I became a scotch drinker Johnny Walker Black. It istoo strong for me now and I drink Red. Have tried Green but no Blue yet.

Only other excitement that summer was an act down the road. I believe it was the Ferndale CountryClub. BelleBarth was the entertainer. She is the filthiest act I have ever seen. Her mouth is worse than Joan Rivers. On my honeymoon in 1952 Belle Barth was working at a bar on 8$^{th}$ st in Miami Beach. I am sorry I gave up the drums. I did play in boot camp but that was the end of my music days

# SPECIAL ACTIVITIES

Home from the mountains and the phone is ringing. One of my club members from the JEMS. "Come right down the club house now"

I was an officer of the club so I figured we had a problem. I could not believe my eyes when I walked in. 5 guys standing in a line. A girl fro my apartment house is sitting in a chair giving everybody blow jobs. I thought it was disgusting but I got on line. We found out a couple of days later that she had contracted syphilis. I immediately got on the trolley and went to my doctor Harry J Cohen on Walton Ave by Yankee Stadium. He took my blood and told me to wait. His daughter and her friends were sitting in the waiting room, I had met them previously. WE were just siting around talking about the summer. Dr. Cohen comes out and in a real loud voice says"Morty your blood is OK but no more fooling around." The girls thought it was funny, I was very embarrassed

I loved that club room on Manor Ave. I always tried to get my dates down there. I remember I once fixed Eric up with a date, friend of my date Bubbie. Big German girl, boy was she built. She had a million excuses why she wouldn't go all the way. Her favorite was that her parents examined her when she came home. Did she think I believed her? Here we are both practically naked, running around and Eric is talking about the Yankees with his date. I wonder if he remembers that night. I know he wasn't always like that, he did take my girlfriend Rhoda away from me.

Eric and Rhoda live in Florida. I flew down for his 75<sup>th</sup> birthday party. He has trouble breathing, so I had to dance with Rhoda the whole night. She still feels good. We are very close even if we do not see each other often. I did take Phyllis to see them when we were down there. She knew both of them from school. I have pictures of the JEMS, Eric and Rhoda's wedding picture. Note sweet sixteen parry picture. It was Janet's party and Eric was her date sitting across from her. Rhoda was my date and we are together. Phyllis is also in the picture 6th one in second row from the left. All the sweet sixteen parties were in the same place. The Village Barn in the Village.

# GETAWAY

Before going into the Navy, I felt I needed a vacation. I called my friend Charlie LaVerdi in Atlantic City. He had a car and he picked me up. Since we were only going for one week, we decided to drive straight through without stopping. We made Miami Beach in 15 hours. We were so proud of ourselves. It was very good timing. No route 95, we had to take 17 and 301. I do remember the only toll was on a bridge in Maryland. We stayed at the Sea and Surf Beach Club, Collins and 16<sup>th</sup> street. One block past the Delano hotel; and two past Wolfie's. Breakfast was a must at Wolfie's. They gave you a big basket of rolls for free. I believe it is gone now, I know the Delano is still there. I went to the Sea and Surf place on my honeymoon, 54 years ago.

Hotel had a social director, Nat Poolgate. I am sure it was not his name. He told me he could fix me up, I believed him, was plenty horny then (Still am) We went to his apartment first,. He brought out a bunch of dirty pictures to show me. Naturally I got hard very fast and before I knew it, I was getting a blow job. My first and only experience with a fag (am I allowed to use that word?) Just as he finished the phone rang, it was the girls and they could not see us. Needless to say I kept away from him the rest of the week. To make matters worse, when I got back to the hotel; there was a towel on my door.... side story.... My daughter in law took Ros and I to a private showing of Dirty Dancing before it opened. The entire small audience was the same age as my daughter in law. When the scene came on with the towel on the door Ros and I started to laugh. The entire audience looked at us strangely. They could not figure out why we were laughing. Will here I am 11pm sitting outside my room. Two girls whom we had met previously came walking by. I explained the situation to them and they said I could sleep in their room, but I had to behave. I can not remember their names. I knew they both lived in the Bronx on Morris Ave and College Ave off 167$^{th}$ St. Going home Charlie and I had $12 total. We knew we could not make it. We invited the girls from the Bronx to go home with us as I lived the Bronx too. We told them they could turn in their plane tickets for a refund. They were smarter than us and didn't turn the tickets in till they got home. They were almost as broke as we were. We ate cheese sandwiches all the way home and slept in one bed and I meant slept. In south Carolina we got pulled over for speeding. Cop said "follow me". He took us to a grocery store where the clerk came out from behind the counter and went into a back room. The court room. We told him we did not have any money and we left him two watches we never did get them back. No other excitement. Charlie went back to Atlantic City. He got married six months later, unfortunately Charlie developed Liver cancer and was gone in six months. His sister Rochetta married Horace the next door neighbor. I know they live in Ventnor. I will look them up. I wonder if she remembers she used to beat him up. Rochetta is in the picture of the Atlantic City girls she is fourth from the right in fist row.

# ANCHORS AWAY

Two of my friends Julie(same one) and Morty D talked me into joining the Naval Reserve with them. Trying to beat the draft. The base was in New Rochelle only 20 minutes away. Reluctantly I did join. My luck, our outfit was short 7 volunteers. They put all the ID's in a hat and pulled out 7. Yep. I won. Only raffle I have ever won. So off to Boot Camp in Bainbridge MD. My buddies felt sorry for me so they took their two week training while I was down there. Picture of both of them with two other friends Eddie Korn and Jerry Collins. Does Eddie Korn ring a bell? Eddie used to chase every fire truck in the neighborhood. We all said he would become a fireman. He did and you may remember a picture of him the newspapers. A ladder across two buildings on fire. He walked the ladder and carried out a lady. Jewish Geography again. Lt Eddie Korn is retired now, he lives in Florida, Place called Coral Lakes in Boynton Beach. My cousin Marilyn lives in the same development ... Back to camp ... I went AOL that weekend and spent it with my friends. Nobody even missed me.

From Boot camp to Storekeepers school in Rhode Island. My adopted brother Norm Landsburg from Calif also signed up for Storekeepers School. He wanted to go to the one in San Diego. I think I tod you the story how he used to go home to my house in the Bronx for the weekend, even when I did not go home. After we graduated from school, we went to Boston for the weekend. We talked my future wife Roslyn and Julie's sister Bernice to come up for the weekend. We had two rooms and neither one of us made out. What a different world it was. We were both very high in the class so we got to pick our next assignments. We both signed up for the Seabees.

Our first tour of duty was to Guantanamo Bay, Cuba. We built the air strip and the barracks for the crews. We must have done a good job as the base is still being used. Different purpose however. The Seabees were al construction workers and very rough guys. Two Jewish boys caught up in this. We did find a Jewish Center in Santiago and we spent a lot of time there. It was a case of Go or fight. One weekend Norm and I and two buddies, Al and Smitty went to Haiti for liberty. We did not have any money so we took cigarettes with us to sell. We checked into the YMCA. Luckily it was on the ground floor. I do not know who came up with the idea but we decided we would become Pimps. We found a young girl in town who wanted to make some extra money. We snuck her in through the window. Smitty and Al had to try her first to see if she was OK. We charged $10 each and gave her 5. We all did OK on that trip. See picture of the 4 of us. Norm is the one in Uniform.

From the warm weather to the cold. Next tour of duty was to Argentea New Foundland. WE built an airstrip there too. It also is still in operation. It was cold. Big sport up there was to try and get your girl to have sex on the snowy hills. I was only slightly successful

I was on a minority term. That meant I only had to serve 21 months. I was discharged from Brooklyn. Norm went back to Calif for discharge and I did see him in Calif once. He was busy telling his daughters about his NY brother. Smitty and Al lived in Jackson Heights. Ros and I used to meet them at a bar where Mickey Mantel and Whitey Ford hung out. Ros was a Yankee fan since she was 7 years old. She left a scrap book. One of the pictures is of Bill Dickey dropping the third strike. You have to be my age to appreciate that.

Navy paid off for me. I went to CCNY for 7 years at night with the government paying forit.

# TYING THE KNOT

Back from the Navy a married man. Oh I forgot to tell you that part of the story. Before I shipped out to Cuba I talked Ros into getting married. Nobody knew about it except one of them en in Ros's office, Ansel. We had the allotment checks going to him. This was so we would have money for our honeymoon. I was a good salesman even then. Ros and I had only one date. I remember we went to The Log Cabin in Armonk NY. We did see a lot of each other before we were married. My friend Julie has a sister Bernice. Ros spent a lot of time at her house as I did too. She gave me a hard time as I am 2 years younger than her. I lived three blocks away. I had her whole family working on her to go out with me, eventually she did. Ros had long pitch black hair. So dark everyone thought she died it. See our Wedding picture. To be perfectly honest, I believe Ros was more in love with my mom than me. She had a terrible life and my mom had nothing but love to give. In fact, Ros moved in with my mom before we were married.

Before I went to Cuba we went to City Hall. We had already had our blood tests, and all the papers We went into Judge Breitel's office. He was not famous then. He looked at our names and said he would not marry us without two Jewish witnesses. Like a maniac I ran around City Hall. I found an elevator operator and a janitor who were Jewish. Was he surprised when I came back to h is office. He was trying to talk us out of it. He married us and the next day I shipped out to Cuba. We did not consummate the wedding. Of course, when I was discharged we were married by a Rabbi. We had two wedding dates but since we didn't consummate the first one we only celebrated the second Jan 10,1952. Can you image I married a virgin.

# *MARRIED LIFE*

Since I did not have a job or a profession, we moved in with my folks. Unfortunately, the first year we were married my mom passed away and Ros' father did also. We had to stay with my father until we got on our feet. He was not the most attentive person. In fact, he cried to us about my mom's hospital bill. Mr Softee pulled him out. My mom was saving money for our first child and we turned that money over to him. Couple of months later my father went to Hawaii with a girl my brother used to take out and when he came home he bought himself a new Chrysler

As soon as we could we moved out. Ros's friend's Leona and Zach brought us to Queens. We moved into Clearview Gardens in Whitestone. A co-op with 1800 families, 95% Jewish. Our rent went from $36 to 74 for an upstairs apartment 3 ½ rooms. We really enjoyed fixing it up.

Our downstairs neighbor was in the same boat, actually worse off. Stan and Marilyn were also newlyweds. Stan was in the accounting field.

His first job was with Leidesdorf, a large accounting firm who paid their employees in the dark. Their name on your resume meant something back then. I was going to CCNY at night and several times during the week they would all eat together at our apartment. We both had our first child there around the same time. Their daughter Ellen and my Eric became good friends. Both loved Mickey Mouse Club, Rumper room, and Miss Jane at Newberry's. Stan was very bright. He passed the first half of the CPA test with a very high, mark. A California firm wanted him to move to there.

51

The firm was Ken Leventhal Assoc. A real Estate firm, Stan was actually his second employee. The firm grew tremendously. Stan eventually became the CEO. At that time they had 1800 employees. I used to love to visit them when I was in Calif. It was always very exciting. I remember once I was in San Francisco and he wanted me to fly down for a party as long as I had a dark suit. The party was at the original Gov Browns's house. All the important people and movie stars were there. He kept introducing me as a Lindsay man from NY. Stan also spoke at the SEC several times. He eventually sold the firm to one of the big 5, Eisner and Luben I think. I also remember a big shot in NY with the stupid hair due, big on casino's was in financial trouble. He called Stan in to NY. They stayed at the Plaza of course. Stan was having breakfast with him when Marilyn came down to join them, She got cold feet and had room service. Can't take the Bronx out of some people. My wife did a lot for their marriage. First time she flew out for their daughter Ellen's Bat Mitzvah, she saw where they were living. Their next door neighbor was the owner of Sony. Ros saw that Marilyn was not keeping up with Stan. She took her shopping and straightened her out. Stan complained but he really appreciated my wife.

Stan never forgot where he came from. He donated 3 million dollars to CCNY for the Stan Ross Accounting Dept. His speech was all about his mom who worked three jobs so he could go to school. I was really very proud of him. He even mentioned Ros and I and the influence we had in his life. We used to see them often but lately we have drifted apart.

My daughter Lesli was also born in the 3 ½ room Apartment. We did move to a larger one before she was 1 year old. For her Bat Mitzvah they gave her a round trip ticket to Calif. Stan had three girls and they really spoiled them all. They took her to San Francisco and stayed at the Top Of The Mart. Thing that impressed Lesli the most was the fact they had a candy store in the room including a soda dispensing machines. The girls also taught her how to use Tampax.

Eric also got a round trip ticket for his Bar Mitzvah. Stan enjoyed him and they did all the boy things

# GROWING PAINS

Eric was a doll, never gave us any major problems. I guess he hid a lot. I know I did find his pot supply. I think I would have worried if he did not try it. He was not the best student. He was smart enough to get through High School without studying. He got out on time without a veery good average. Went to University of Buffalo. Never asked to go to a private school. I remember when he graduated, he handed the diploma to his mom. "Here Mom this is for you" I know he is sorry now he did not take college seriously, He was always a very hard worker. In High School he came home one day and told us he was going to work after school. WE told him his job was school and we didn't want him traveling to work. He fooled us, job was down the block at the steak restaurant. On Utopia Parkway. He kept his marks up and we could not stop him. He started as a kitchen helper, went to bus boy and eventually waiter. Only thing bad about this job was the restaurant was owned by Steve Rubel and Ian Schrager and Neil Schlessenger who ran the place. Since they had an IN, every night they ended up at Studio 54.

Eric has his own family two boys Remy and Alex and he still works very hard. I am sure proud of him. He is a real street smart business man. Rest of the story later on.

Lesli was another story. She had her own way of doing things from day 1. Boy did she have a temper … still does. She had a habit of holding her breath and passing out. She once locked her self in the bathroom and refused to open the lock She started crying and then you heard a thump. Ros and I were at our wits end. The Dr did tell us she would come around by herself. We called a neighbor Herb, he came running over and said to Lesli ... "Lesli I have the biggest present you ever saw" Click she opened the door. "Where is my present." she made up for all the anxiety she gave us. Lesli became a Nurse, she would have stayed with it but she wanted her own family. She kept her license up and eventually became the Risk Manager for Long Island Jewish Hospital. We always appreciate her, but when Ros got sick we were so proud of the respect she got from all the big shots in the hospital. Her two daughters Danielle and Dara were also very proud of her. Lesli went for her masters and graduated Suma Cum Laudi with straight A's.

Lesli is a single parent. She works very hard and sometimes long hours. Her girls are still very proud of her.

# WORK, WORK, WORK

By the time we moved to Clearview I had already had three different jobs. Macy's of course for Christmas. One of my jobs was at Wormser Hats. Believe it or not men wore hats, I had to wear one every day. Since I did not pay for them I did. One of Ros's friends Deli(Sydelle) got me the job. I used to go out to lunch with the shipping dept. My boss the Sales Manager called me into his office one day. He told me to always go out to lunch with a higher group than you are. Never forgot that lesson. I did too. My brother-in-law Ira when an opening came at Emerson Radio he got me a job as an expediter. I eventually moved up to Jr Buyer in the Military Dept. My boss Ernie Sonders came back into my life 30 years later. He married another friend of Ros's. From that side of the fence I got into sales. I joined a Manufacturers Representative firm owned by Harry Finkelstein. One man operation with two secretaries. I learned a lot form him. He had 6 lines and they all fit together. Sold all 6 lines tothe same customers. In those days TV was just coming out. NY was loaded with set manufacturers CBS, Dumont, Fada, Pilot Radio, Magnavox, Olympic, Emerson, Carlton Stewart and probably more that I can not remember. Harry sold them the mask for the front, glass panel, fabricated back, plastic cup over tube end, and two different hardware lines. When I joined him he told me to go out and find my own Industry. Boy was I scared. I lucked out. If you remember, Long Beach or maybe it was called Atlantic Beach was just starting to build the BeachClubs. Capri, Atlantic Beach club, Sands, and two others. Our glass line was Hamilton Glass. I think they are still in business in Chicago. Electrical Contractor took a liking to me and

I got asll the jalousy doors and mirrors in each cabana. It was a big order and gave me a lot of confidence. I also learned a good tool from Harry. I was there about a year when he called me into his office. He said name your 10 biggest customers, their spouces names children's names and their birthdays. I thought he was nuts, But I remembered it. It was a very good sales tool. My sister-in-law Ira's wife used to rent a cabana at Capri. She would taske my son Eric with her. He was a Ham, At 6 he knew the pledge of Allegiance and had to say it to everyone he saw. He still is a ham.

I worked for three other Rep firms before getting involved with a Wasp. Ballou Inc. This was a second generation firm, a rarity at that time. His father left him the business. They had one primary line Heinemann Electric. This line paid all the bills and left plenty over. Heinemann makes a circuit breaker that has to be used in all Military items as well as all sophisticated Electronic equipment like IBM and Western electric. For example. These breakers are not affected by heat but by the electrical load they carry. No competition at that time. Bill had three outside salesmen, one inside salesmen and two secretaries. Inside man was a retired ITE person. Who took care of all technicasl problems and entered the orders. John was in his late 60's when I met him.

He traveled by bus and train everyday from Ridgewood NY to Ridgewood NJ. It must have taken him at least two hours. each way. He smoked a pack of Fatima cigarettes and drank a pint of Fleishman's daily. He also had a much younger wife Kitty she was a knock out. John passed away when he was in his 80's.

All the salesmen were graduated Engineers. I was hired as the sales manger. The firm needed a peddler, that wasme. First thing I did was give them all a test. you guest it.… Name your 10 best customers, etc. Bill was the only one who knew some of the answers. He only had two customers IBM and Western Electric(That's Bell labs and AT&T)' If anyone wanted to crack these two accounts they had to talk to Bill. Reason I am telling you about his power, as that is how we got big lines. I was the salesmen in the negotiations Bill was the engineer. He was a good engineer but he couldn't sell his way out of a paper bag.

Line I enjoyed the most was ASEA. A Swedish firm as large as GE except no home appliances. The part of the line we had was the Contactors and Starters. Contactors are big relays priced from $500 to $2500 each. Starters are a combination of the contactor and an attachment to protect against overloads. It seems the Swedish government taxes all profits at a very high rate. Asea spent large amount of money promoting their line. They brought 20 representative firms to Sweden for training Bill was divorced and did not tell me the wives were invited too. Ros never forgave him for it. First thing they did was bring us to Stockholm for a weekend of R &R. They gave us a card to identify us by. Anywhere you went in Stockholm you just signed your name. That included the whore houses which were very prevalent there. First night three Ameri can couples, Bill, myself and one of the sales managers and his wife went out together. We went to a night club, I think it was Maxim's. Ima the sales mangers wife got up to dance with someone from another table, not in our group. She came back and told her husband she was going to leave withtheman she was dancing with, and she would see him in the morning. He said OK see you tomorrow. You had to see the expressions on the American wives. I think it took 10 minutes before they closed their mouths. Swedish people thought nothing of it. The next night just 4 single men went out with another sales person from the firm. This was a young guy who had been to the States. He told us where he was taking us. You will not believe the nightclub he took us to. I know I will never forget it. I have seen women having sex with a dog.... but never with a horse ... The big sportin Stockholm is to get your date to have sex on the Palace Wall. I now know why the all wore long skirts. I remember I saw the movie "I am curious Yellow"

They showed this sport in the movie. Thank God it was only for the weekend. They took us to the plant about an hour and half away for training. This was in May when it is light all the time. Trainingwas for 5 day. I have never been wined and dined by anyone like this trip. Every night was a party. The even had a photographer for us, who was busy taking pictures everynight. They gave us a phot album. I hope I can find it to include in my book. Before we left the States they assigned us to individual families who had children same as we did. WE were to bring gifts for the kids. I was assigned to a family with children same age as mine. I brought Yankee shirts and hats and they were a big success. I had to sleep in their house one night. His wife was gorgeous, blond of course Most of the women were all knockout. Breakfast she comes down with a white sheer robe with nothing under it. It was hard eating breakfast. Their final gesture, they took us to the Orefus factory. Gave us gifts to take home. They then deposited us back in Stockholm for a weekend of fun. Next year the meeting was in Pt St Lucie Florida. The American wives jumped all over Ros."How did you Have the nerve to send him to Sweden alone" I still blush when ever anyone mentions Sweden. At the dinner party I told Ros not top dance with any of the factory people. Unless you want to know if they are lefty or righty. You do not understand? The President of ASEA came and asked Ros to dance. She came back to the table her face was bright Red. She said you are right he is a lefty. They are very sensuous people, they hold you so tight you can feel which side his penis is on. ASEA eventually merged with Brown Boveria another large European company. They are listed on the NYStock Exchange ABB is their letters.

While at Ballou we starteda manufacturing firm. IPC Automation with a brilliant engineer Bob Boyd. We were all equal partners. Bob's forte was solid state controls. Bill had him building products for IBM and Western Electric. I had him designing products for the Elevator Industry. Like Bill was to IBM I was to Otis in Yonkers. I even had my own parking space. Space came about as I was always giving the guards tickets to sports events. Needless to say we wqere very successful. We eventually sold IPC to one of our big customers. Bob went to work for them and I started my own Rep firm with the IPC line.

While working for Ballou, I knew he would never give mepart of the Rep firm. I convinced Bill into letting me start a distributor business with his lines for a start. I would run the business in Whitestone whereI lived and I would take John Reardon intothe firm so he would not have that crazy trip to NJ every day. The firm Power electro Supply co. PESCO started to grow. John had passed away at this time and I convinced my son Eric to come in and run the firm. He did not like the agreement I had with Bill as he more or less had final say even though we were equal partners. Our original plan was to build the firm up to entice a firm in Philadelphia area who could compliment our lines. The Philadephia firm had 6 locations but non in the NY area. Eric was anatural and he built the firm up to the I million dollar level. At this point you have to bring in more management or sell the firm. Eric contacted the Philadelphia firm I/O Corp. Frank Keller was the CEO. They were very interested and made an appointment to come up to NY a week later. Bill Mushum was the money man I remember his wife owned oe of the big desgner outfits. I think it was Jordache or something at that level. Eric was very sharp. He went to a fancy restaurant in Whitestone Café on the Green and set it up with the manager. I can just see the scene. Oh good afternoon Mr Lynn, your Table is ready. Brought Eric a drink and then asked them what they would like. Even I would have been impressed. At the end of the meal they just left without even getting a check. They went back to the office and went through the books. Eric told them what he was asking and they said they would get back to him.

I think he asked for 1 million cash. Within a week they called Eric and told him they would givehim $600,000 cash within 30 days. The three of us got together and thought it was a good offer. Eric told them we would accept it. While the lawyers were writing it up Bill called me to have dinner with him. He said the business was doingvery well and he would buy me out. That was in our original agreement. I said what about Eric? He said Eric is smart he will get another job. Bill had two useless sons who were going to run the firm. I was furious but there was nothing I could do about it. My fault fornot going to a lawyer with the agreement. Eric talked Bill into giving him a big bonus and he would stay and train his sons. He was very smart my son. He did not even seem upset. I was ashamed of myself. Eric did help his son and then said good by. What Ericdid not tell us was that he Philadelphia firm was more interested in him than the business. They told him to start another firm in NY with a blank check. Eric started I/O of NY. Eventually they moved him to Phila. To run the entire operation. He eventually bought out the other owners. Absentee management was not the best deal and he sold off all the divisions. He even sold off the Philadelphia operation. Eric was offered a position at Alliance Holding where he still works. He does a lot of traveling but he loves his job. Moral of this story, Do not think you are smarter than the next guy.

# VACATION TIME

We were a typical family and took normal vacations. We were not rich, but we had to get away during the summer.

Our most interesting vacation was when we went to Israel. I was there before. I was always active with the youth in my neighborhood. I managed baseball and basketball teams. My Temple, Clearview Jewish Center always had a strong basketball team. We played all over. Isreal invited us to play in their Macabee games for their 25th anniversary. Only 4 teams from the US were invited. Ros remembered Sweden, insisted I take my son Eric with me. Eric was 12 the team players were all 17-18. I think she sent Eric to watch over me. We no sooner landed in Israel when the boys went to work. I know one boy Richard was wearing red boots when we landed. Next time I saw him he had the biggest water pipe I ever saw. Within ½ hour they all had water pipes. One guy sold his dungarees. Weather was the coldest May they ever had. They put us up at the Wingate Institute. To far to walk to the town of Natanya. The other American teams complained since there was no heat at the Institute and they moved their teams to town. I was afraid to move my boys. I wanted them to play basketball. All the teams were championship teams. Newburg NY was our rival We played them several scrimmage games and beat them most of the time. In the tournament we had to play Israel's number 1 team. We beat them in overtime. We did loose to Israel's second team. At the final games the teams were exchanging shirts. I had bought my team new uniforms and they refused to give them up and just shook hands Touring of course was great. Only problem I had was in the Carmel Winery. They all came out drunk. Wasn't bad enough with the drugs, I had to watch them with wine too. In Jerusalem they all bought fleece jackets. I think half of them had the bugs in them. We made it home with good memories.

Different story when I went with Ros. It was our 25$^{th}$ anniversary. Lets see that was 1977. We no sooner sat down on the plane when the lady next to me spilled a soda all over my pants. She refused to wipe it off. Just joking. Needless to say she was very embarrassed. We got friendly with them Arlene and Stanley. We are still friends except Ros and Stanley are gone. I talk to Arlene every once in a while. They moved to ScottsdaleAZ and we did see them several times. I will never forget that trip. Arlene and Ros managed to find a jewelry factory in Tel Aviv. Stanley and I found the Red light district two blocks past the Dan hotel. Shonda, Jewish girls sitting in the windows with big Chai's on. We also discover in Haifa you can tell when the wine is bad. Never thought I would know the difference. Stanley ordered Mateus, what could go wrong … After three bottles we changed to an Israeli wine. Israel is a place everyone should visit just to see what a country could do with the Barren land. Arabs living in Jerusalem have it much better than Arabs living elsewhere in the Arab world. Regardless what the NY Times says

Only other different vacation was the one to England. We flew over. Two other couples with us. They both got cheap at the wrong time. For $700 more we could have flown on the Concord. I am a pisha compared to these two couples. One was the chief engineer at CBS, other was a dentist with mucho real estate property in Whitestone. We of course did all the shows. Real tourists and did all the side trips. Highlight of the trip was the trip home on the QE2. Very exciting. Ocean was not cooperative however and was a rough crossing. Ros liked lamp chops and she had them three times a day.

We did a lot of traveling in the US after each Elevator Show. We also managed to see Ireland, Scotland and Italy before children. Ireland was really fun. We went on a pub tour and stayed at Castles. Even managed to kiss the Blarney Stone

# ON MY OWN

I started my own Representative firm in 1987. I had IPC Automation which made solid state products for the Elevator Industry. I learned from my days with Harry Finkelstein and I went after lines that could all be sold to the Elevator Trade. I was able to add three lines. Ajax Transformer, which made large units mostly. Size will give you an idea of this product line. The typical unit was 2feet by 4feet by 6feet tall in metal cases. You needed a fork lift truck to move them. Every elevator has one of these Isolation Transformers and all DC jobs have a choke the same size. I added Milwaukee Resistor, their units typically were 6 inches long. My last line was Cougar electronics in Brooklyn. They manufactured selenium rectifiers, if you ever smelled burnt eggs in an elevator it was probably a bad rectifier. Cougar knew their product was going out of style and they became a distributor for solid state rectifiers and Diodes.

I insisted on the same territory for all my lines. This was a first in the Industry My territory was North America, nice eh, certainly big enough. Actually I only had 30 potential customers in the entire territory.

I was doing what I enjoyed, did not have to answer to anyone except my VP and Treasurer, Ros my wife.

The NY territory was a big part of the business. Eight customers which included Otis and Schindler(Westinghouse old name). We got very friendly with these customers and to this day I can call most of them my friends. I have been to their family affairs and they have been to mine. Rest of the territory was not as easy. The largest potential customer was Motion Control Engineering in Sacramento Calif.

Home also of elevator Controls where they came from. Owners of MCE were two brothers Javad and Majid. Iranian Shiite Muslims. Being Jewish I was very concerned. Ros and I went out to visit them on a Thursday. We took both brothers and their families out to dinner on different nights. We hit it off immediately. Still had to get my products designed into their Con troller's. Other firm Elevator Controls was also owned by two Mexican brothers. Took them all out together and hit it off with them as well.

The Industry has a trade show every year which we exhibited at. They also entertained the mates when the show was on. I must give Ros the credit for a lot of our success, would tell her which wife to get close to and make sure they came with their husbands to our booth.

She was great and everyone loved her. Like all organizations the old timers were very cliquish. Ros saw that they wee ignoring the wife of Elevator Controls. She sat with her and brought her into the crowd.

Fernando her husband never forgot it. Roslyn also became very friendly with Shirin the wife of Javad. We are still very close. When their daughter Sarah got married we were the only elevator friends who were invited. Make sure you see pictures of my booths and formal dinner party where we are with the two Rahaminians with their wives.

Ros and I continued going out of town on Thursday, seeing customers onFriday and romancing them on the weekend. Dallas Texas, Chicago Il, Richmond Va., Memphis Tn. Mankato MN, as well as Los Angeles Calif. Were the locations of our other customers. We had three good customers in Canada Toronto and Montreal, so we joined their organization too. We exhibited at their show as well. We could not have been happier, and we were making good bucks.

Our success must have gotten around as we got a call from a firm in Seatle Wa. They were invited to make a presentation at Schindler in Morristown NJ. Schindler besides buying Westinghouse had also bought my biggest customer O. Thompson in NY. Sweo was the Seatle firm. They manfactured a drive. This is the product that makes the elevator go up and down. I told them I would make the presentation, but if I was successful I wanted the line same as my other lines Sweo only had one elevator account MCE and they wanted to keep it as a house account. Needless tosay I did a good job and they gave me the line. I had the owners of MCE call them and I got the account at a reduced commission. It was a perfect fit. We immediately flew to Seattle. I wanted to learn their line and meet the important people. We went all went out to dinner with their wives but this time the factory picked up the check Best part of the line was that it was a 10% commission rate same as IPC. Sweo's [products sold from $2500 to $8000 each. I was also very lucky as my only competition on this line was from GE. Their salespeople could not be bothered with the elevator trade. No volume.

Largest customer did about 800 units a year. I was very successful in getting their drives into everyone of my customers. Within 4 months my commission checks were in 5 figures and they did not always start with a 1.

Things were too good, something had to happen. Sweo sold out to Baldor motors a very largefirm listed on the NY Stock Exchange. Baldor has offices with big staffs all over the States and the rest of the world. They immediately fired all the Sweo Reps except me. I immediately got on a plane and flew to Ft Smith Ar. Not an easy place to get to. Fly to Dallas and take a puddle jumper to Ft Smith. Foolishly I went alone. I did bring 2 dozen bagel with me instead of Ros. I met with the President and VP of Marketing. They were glad I came and enjoyed the bagels. I asked them how come they fired everyone but me. President Wally called his secretary and had her bring in two charts. Charts showed my sales growth and profit level.(seems their sales force was always cutting prices) Both my lines went straight up. Wally said as long as your lines keep going the same way, you do not have to worry I immediately responded, "My wife is very nervous, can you put that in writing"

"Don't be silly this is a very large firm we are listed on the stock exchange" I thanked them and went home and immediately started to prepare for the loss of this line. I lasted a whole year. This was odd as Baldor had a big office in NJ 8 outside salesmen and a staff of 5 inside.

The last elevator Show that I had Baldor, I had a contest going to win a Cammero Car(toy of course) you had to identify how many booths had my drives in their controllers. I had everyone of the Controller manufacturers using my drives Factory people were very impressed but they still terminated me. I got even with them and made sure all my customers switched to another drive manufacturer. Magnatek got the business. I did visit them but they just picked my brain. Baldor eventually stopped showing at the Eevator Show as they had none of the business. I can give you a very good tip on a stock, Baldor, BEZ on the NYSTock Exchange. 95% of the stock is owned by district managers. If they sell the stock they would loose the line. Merrill Lynch makes a market for the stock. I bought it in a street name at 17 sold it at 34 and split 2 for 1. I did this twice. Eventually sold 600 shares from my original 100. Today the stock is going wild and I do not know why but it is way up

Shows were the most fun. We exhibited at, NAEC, CECA, and NAVTP. Last one is the Consultants who write the specs. They are very powerful. If they put you in the spec nobody is going to use anything else. I remember many years ago, NYC Housing specs were written by NY firm on 42nd ST. Engineer in charge liked my solid state starter from IPC. He put it in the Specs. City housing has 3500 elevators and they change 10% A YEAR. That was 350 starters at

$500 each. Unfortunately technology changed and the drives became AC which did not need my starter. Ros also loved to work the booth. We always had give aways for the ladies.

After the conventions we always went on vacation. Usually with a couple of couples and sometimes with a big group. We went to Hong Kong twice with big groups, stops in Singapore, Japan and Hawaii. See pictures of Hong Kong Group WE spent a whole week there before China took over. Ros and I love to shop and did we have a ball. See pictures of the Rahaminians dressed in Chinese Garb like royalty.

As you can see we were veryclose with the Rahaminians. Javad's wife was picked for him by his parents. First time he saw her was at the wedding. It worked out fine as they are a very happy couple. They have three children 2 girls and a boy. Youngest daughter Sabra used to sit on my lap when we visited them. She is too big for that now. Oldest daughter Sarah I told you about her wedding. She married a WASP from New England. His first job out of college was with Yahoo before they went public. They gave him stock for signing on. Do not have to tell you the rest of the story. Never will forget the wedding. So many of their customs are the same as mine. They hold a canopy over the bride and groom. Every women comes up and puts a stitch in it. They told me it is to keep the mother-in-laws mouth shut. Majid picked his own wife Miryam. They have three beautiful girls. We have watched them grow up into fine ladies. We used to make sure we spent equal time with both families. Both have apartments in NYC we used to see them often.

A little late, but what do you know about the elevator business. I know it has its ups and downs. Market is broken into two segments, New Construction and Modernization. New construction belongs to the big boys. Otis, Schindler, Kone etc do all their own work on new installations Modernization uses controllers made by MCE and other. Modernization is probably 200 times bigger than new installations. Even Otis offices when they are doing modernization will buy from firms like MCE. Incidently MCE has about 70% of the market.

I told you about the yearly NAECconvention. My Swan song was about two years ago. The convention was in Orlando. Brand new hotel Gaylord Palms a copy of Opryland in Nashville butmore plush. Convention rate was $275 a night. We had three rooms. My grandchildren had a ball. They could go anywhere in the hotel and sign for anything. My oldest grandson Remy wants to know when we are going back and this time he wants to being his girlfriend

# *MY ROS*

Ros was very poor. I do not know if her friends realized how poor she was. Their parents did as they were always feeding her. I guess they did know her status as for her sweet sixteen they bought her a blouse. Rest of the girls got jewelry or perfume. Ros' best friend was Deli, real name Sydelle. She married Bob Romm from out of the neighborhood. Wonder how she met him? Oh, I know her sister Anita introduced them. After all he was from the West Bronx he must have had money. Bob passed away at an early age. The Romm's were involved in the entertainment business. Bob's father at one time was head of William Morris. Agency. Bob also was an agent. Bob once took Zack to a rehearsal, Frank Sinatra came walking down the isle. He stopped at Bob and said "hello Mr Romm". Bob said, Hi Frank. Zack told me the story and I believe it. Zack married Leona from around the corner, Boynton Ave to Ward Avenue Leona is next to Sydell in the picture from my grandson Alex's Bar Mitzvah. Next to Leona is Elayne then than Gloria, May Florence and Rita. Do they look 76? See picture of 6 of the girls when they were girls.

How many can you match up? Florence's Family owned the shoe store on Westchester Ave. Sterns shoes. She got divorced when her kids were all grown up and went back to school. She became a NYC School teacher. She must have been very dedicated as she worked in Bed/Sty. Her new husband Jerry is our resident plumber. He helped everybody out. He is retired now and he wears a tee shirt that says … "I'm Retired Now Call A Plumber" Rita married Larry, not even around the corner, same street other side on Ward Ave. I guess they were all to cheap to buy gas.

Elayne married Morty a neighborhood dentist. All the girls had a crush on him but she pursued him and didn't give them a chance or him either. Morty was 10 years older than her. Elayne was a dance teacher and she worked on Morty until he was as good as her. Her new partner Gene has two left feet, but she is working on him too. He is the man in the same picture. Let's see who did I forget ... Gloria, her fame was her sister Dianne who was one of my friends. Gloria is the one who gave me Phyllis' number when I left Florida in 2006. May is also in the picture. I do not know where her husband Milty came from but I'll bet it was in the same neighborhood. One couple is missing Renee and Sam. Renee got chest pains the day of the Bar Mitzvah and was afraid to make the trip to Pa. Sam is our resident poet. We take each other out for birthday's and anniversaries. Sam writes a poem about them. Last line of each paragraph is always the same and we all chant it. Oh Veh. OH Veh When I took everyone out to dinner at Alex's affair we drank a toast to Renee and Sam honoring friendships and we all chimed in Oh Veh Oh Veh. There is nothing like good friends. I am sure everyone was thinking about Ros. she was there in spirit.

These girls stayed close even after they got married. All lived near each other in Queens. Now they are all retired, they still live near each other. Three live in Florida full time, 4 go down for the winter. They. Usually see each other at least every Sat morning. During the week as well. They are a special group. Friends from Public School P.S. 93 on Boynton on to High School at Monroe three blocks up on Boynton. They are thicker than family. Actually, they are family. Zack made Leona a 60th birthday party at the Water Club in NY He only wanted to invite close family. Of course all the girls were invited. Leona and Zack are the ones who brought us to queens. Their claim to fame was their downstairs neighbor was Ed Roman from CCNY. I am sure you remember the story. Before I took the basketball team to Israel we had a fund raiser. Basketball game between my team and a pick up team. Ed Roman, Phil Jackson, Willis Ried, and the Weinstein boys.(Boys had tried out for the Nicks but didn't make it.) We slaughtered them.... you do not believe it? How about buying a bridge.

# TRUE CONFESSIONS

I am sure my children Eric, Lesli and Janet will read this book. I may have to leave them a free copy. Oh what they must think of their father. Only one thing they have to remember, I might not have been the perfect father or husband but we all do the best we can. It's ironic, whenever we get together and start talking about the past, my children only remember what I did wrong. Lesli remembers I used to call her crisco (fat in the can) I realize now my humor was in bad taste. She is much smarter with her girls. My son now knows why I carried on when I took him for a sport jacket. Murray's was having a sale. The one on sale made his rear end stick out. All I said, was you have a big ass. At that time I am sure he didn't realize I could afford the one on sale, not the one we ended up buying. My grandson's will not have that problem my son does very well and he can buy them anything they want. As far as a husband, I was not the best, I also wasn't the worst. We had our ups and downs. One thing I was faithful throughout our marriage. I had plenty of opportunity to do otherwise. My motto was I would only do things I would want my wife to do. Yeh I was a little bosy. Things had to be done my way. Ros felt it was easier than fighting with me. Our friends thought I was a good husband. Always helped in the house. The truth of the matter is I had to be in control. Nobody was permitted o to load the dishwasher(Hm I see Lesli is the same way) I cannot apologize for any of my past actions. I will try to be a better Father and Grandfather.

# FIRST DIVIDEND

If you ask my kids where and when we took them on vacation, they would both tell you we never did. They almost have me convinced. I do remember we went upstate NY visited all the forts and the Finger Lakes.

Another year we went to Williamsburg VA. Kids loved it because in those days if you were in the complex the kids could go all over by themselves by bus … By coincidence we met one of Ros's friends with their kids and they hung out together. May and Milty I know they had a ball. We also took them to Sturbridge Mass. Old style Village. We of course took them to Hershey Pa. In those days you could go through the factory and see the big vats of chocolate. They also got a kick out of the Amish country. Good and Plenty and town of Intercourse. I can't think of other vacations but I am sure we took them away. My poor underprivileged children.

For 5 years every Christmas week we went to a small hotel in Kerhonksen. It was Rubens. Everything was done in the main building so you always knew where your children were. We all loved it. The first year we went the hotel sat us with three other couples. We hit it off immediately. I said since we are having so much fun we should do it in the city as well. I told them Ros was having a 20<sup>th</sup> reunion from her high school. When I told them the school they all burst out laughing. Two of the women graduated with Ros. Our kids were 5 and 8 at the time. Its over 35 years and I am still very friendly with them. Rhoda and Bill live in NJ a retirement village. Greenbrier. Arnie and Bea live up in Pamona NY. WE try and go away for three or four days every year. Other couple moved to Arizona. Nothing like old friends.

At the same time we were in the mountains for Christmas week we rented a Bungalow for the summer. G & S Bungalows in Mountaindale. NY. Three Jewish couples and the rest were Italian. My Saxophones player Danny had been going there before we did. Every Friday night was Feast night. The women cooked all week long and we ate like pigs. We also drank too much. Good thing we only had to walk home. My daughter learned how to play spin the bottle. Reason I know, was they used a Clorox bottle and she was always coming home with stains on her pants. WE continued going till the kids were old enough for sleep away camp.

Both Lesli and Eric went to Cedjwin Camp in Port Jervis. They both made some very good friends whom they still see. They continued going until the went to College.

Finally both off to college. We bought a small two bedroom house in a town near Monroe NY, Washingtonville. The winery owners were a very well connected and you never had to worry about crime. We had it for 9 years. first couple of years the kids were not allowed to come. We sold the house because the town was getting crowded. We once had to wait two lights toget into town. Sold it to a young couple with two kids. Husband took the bus in Monroe to NY every day.

Back home in Whitestone and no place to run away to. One of our Temple friends Murray and Millie kept bugging us to come out to their place in the Hampton's. Just look. We were never there. We took a ride out one weekend and immediately fell in love with the place. They lived in a small condo, only 46 units .9 of a mile to town and same to the beach. I was a beach boy from the start and Ros loved it too. Murray and Millie were very friendly with 5 couples. We lucked out, as they took us into their group. Four Jewish couples and an Indian(from India) and a wasp. What a combination. Mohan worked for NYC Parks Dept. He was an Assistant Commissioner., am sure if he wasn't Indian he would have been the commissioner. He is very bright and knows about everything. Even my Phyllis was impressed with him. Joyce his wife was a school teacher in the NYC School System. After a couple of years, she did not find it rewarding enough and she went to work for the School of the Deaf. I am sure she took a cut in pay. She is that kind of person. Some of the other couples have been friends since their children were young growing up in Flushing. They are really unbelievable. Every weekend someone makes a happy hour. Nobody gets insulted if you do not come. If you have company they expect you to bring them along. No pressure, No fuss, just clean fun. Same for Dinner if you want to join them its fine if not do your own thing. As Rush Limbar would say"More Fun Than A Person Should BE allowed To have" I am sure I am the only one who listens to him. They think I am a Republican(Dirty word)

Canterbury Mews is the name of the place. We have our own tennis courts. Irving is our tennis pro. In other words he knows how to hold the racket. Usually every weekend we have games. I had not played in 30 years They sure made fun of my racket. Bought a new one and Irving would practice with me all week long. He is getting me ready to play McEnroe. John's parents live with us. Patrick comes around but I have only seen John's children. For a small community we had our share of celebrities. Balenchine used to own one of the units as did one of his dancers. We also had a Japanese Designer who built the statues in Lincoln Center. He sold his place abut 5 years ago. My favorites are the owners of Mirko's restaurant in Water Mill. If you do not know it, you do not eat in fine restaurants in the Hampton's. It's number 1 in my book. Only one that comes close is the American Hotel in Sag Harbor. Mirko's live right near me. See picture of all 5 couples from Canterbury. Starting on the left as you can easily see Mohan and Joyce, Murray and Millie,

Warren and Mimi, Ros and I, other friends Ed and Frances and last Bruce and Doris.

Comes the winter and everyone runs away. The Hampton's get deserted. Ros and I had been going to Florida for the last 8 years. Went to Scottsdale AZ once too. Jan. Feb and March

# BACK HOME

While in Florida in March 2005, Ros spit up blood. We thought it was her allergies. She happened to mention it on the phone to Lesli. Lesli got very excited and said" pack up and come home now. I will expect you in my house by Wed" This was Monday, we were half packed already, she scared us and we did as she asked. We made it to her house by Wednesday. Lesli had scheduled us to see a group of Doctors in her hospital. LIJ. She also scheduled us to see the Oncology heads at NY Hospital, Sloan Kettering, and North Shore. Ros was diagnosed with Lung Cancer stage 3A. We later found out 3B is fatal. Ros like the trooper she was did the Chemo and Radiation treatment first. The lump did not shrink enough. Never heard a complaint from her. Doctors told us only definitive way was to remove the lung. Ros did not even blink, she said let's go for it. Dr Kline in LIJ was going to do the operation. He told us there was a 30% chance Ros would not get off the table because of her age. I know Ros did not care, Her biggest fear in life was to suffer and linger with Cancer

Ros came through the operation in good shape. In fact they discharged her in 5 days. This was Oct 2005

My daughter-in-law Janet always made Thanksgiving. One time of the year she really cooked. Just joking.... We all went down to Pa. Lesli and her girls. Riley the dog and us. Meal as usual was perfect. Friday Ros said she did not feel good. She had developed a fever and we went right to the hospital LIJ. Leslie had set everything up ahead of time. From the emergency room we went right to ICU unit. Ros had developed Pneumonia. They did everything they could but, her

kidney shut down and it was over. Ros passed away on Nov 29,2005
The world lost a good person …

# LIFE GOES ON

After 54 years of marriage what do you do? My family took it very hard. I could not believe my granddaughters, they both spoke at Ros's funeral service. Eric and Lesli did too. Only request Ros had given me ahead of time was that she wanted to buried as an Orthodox Jew and she wanted Rabbi Simon top officiate. Rabbi Simon did officiate, he was scheduled to fly to Florida but he changed his tickets. This funeral chapel did something differently, they taped the service. Boy am I glad, I did not hear Anything at the services. I have played the tape several times. We had 18 cars going to the Cemetery in New Jersey. Of course some got separated and didn't make it but they were all therein spirit. We were very fortunate, we had so many good friends and family..Still have them.

Two weeks later you find yourself all alone in the house. I have a good crew in the Hampton's but at night you are still alone. Mad as hell. We planned on going together. You have to live through it to know what it is like. You can let it get the best of you and become a couch potato or move on. The pain never goes away, you relive all the memories, however life goes on.. I elected to keep myself as busy as I could.

Since we usually went to Florida in the winter, Mid January I drove down by myself. Stopped at all the same spots we always did. And lived every year over again. I knew Lesli and the girls would fly down Presidents week. It was a tradition already. Unfortunately my grandson's did not get the same time off.. I must thank Ros for her friends. Five of them are widows and they kept me very busy. When ever I went to dinner I had a harem. None of them wanted to sleep over though. We once went to the same restaurant twice in one week. We got the same waiter. He pulled me aside and wanted to know what the story was.I told him I was their pimp, and to let me know if he is interested in any of them.He said he would but didn't. Played a lot of Golf and Tennis Leona was my partner most of the time. One of the Hampton couples, Irving and Shirley have a placein Del Ray and they kept me busy too. Irving likes to cook and the price was right.

Upon returning to the Hampton's, I decided to make myself very busy. I had Irving and Murray for Tennis during the week and Mohan and Joyce joined us on the weekends (they still live in Bayside). Took some computer courses at the Library. Trying to catch up to my grandchildren. Joined a play reading group,and joined a swing dancing club. Ros and I used to love to dance. At thistime Murray and Millie moved out to the Hampton's full time. They keep me informed on all that is happening in town. Something was still missing. I think I told you Ros' friend Gloria before I left Florida gave me the name of an old girlfriend from Public School. She was divorced for many years and lived in Princeton NJ3.5 hours away. I called her and made a date for lunch in Princeton. After a few minutes it was like we saw each other last week. Now you know how Phyllis got into the picture. I will leave it alone for now. Who knows what the future will bring. Group in the Hampton's usually go out to eat on the weekend.I had been the odd person. One of the women Mimi is a widow. Her husband Warren passed away couple of years ago. We all miss him, he was a fun person.I wish I had known him when he was in his prime. I understand he was quite a ball player. A lot of times we go out as a couple Mimi and I we split the bill. She is a lot of fun. Very smart, knows about everything, including relationships. She teachers at an all boys Yeshiva. They put the lights out when they pay her. I think it's a labor of love. Have a few other women I go out with, one is in my play reading group. We went out a few times, she is good company but I do not believe anything will develop. I continue going to Temple Saturday morning, as I did with Ros. I find it very restful. I have also been seeing a couple of ladies from the Temple. I figure four in the Hampton's, one in old neighborhood who is divorced and Leona should keep me busy. I also intend to see more of Phyllis. Can not figure out why I am so comfortable with her.

I know as long as I keep myself very busy I will be OK.

I hope you have enjoyed my stories. I am sure you all have your own. You have to live every day like tomorrow is your last as some day you will be right. Last picture is of my entire Family. I am sure you can recognize my daughter Lelsi's boyfriend Gary

enjoy.

**Every book has an Index. Not this one. This one has a thank you list.**

**First my wife Ros for the 54 years we had together, and for putting up with me.**

Next I thank my children Eric and Lesli and Janet of course for giving me four beautiful grandchildren to love and watch grow up. Remy, Alex, Danielle, and Dara. You have enriched my life.

Friends and relatives also play a good part in your life, I thank them too.

I must also thank Phyllis. I probably would not have gone for therapy if it wasn't for her.

Last but not least, I must thank my therapist Harriet Vogel. She showed me how to become a whole person. I know she will say I did all the work. Harriet had me make a list of a ll the things I am thankful for and whenever I get low I just pull out the list. It works. Try it.

Thank you for taking the time to read my book. Life is short and we have to grab it all in. I hope you do not mind my poor English and all the spelling errors. English was my worst subject

morty

978-0-595-46513-2
0-595-46513-7

www.ingramcontent.com/pod-product-compliance
Lightning Source LLC
Chambersburg PA
CBHW051256050326
40689CB00007B/1213